The Miracle Learning System!™

Learn How to Learn

Aamir M. Muhammad

AMM Publishing Company
Lawrence, Kansas

The Miracle Learning System!™
Learn How to Learn

Publisher: AMM Publishing Company
P.O. Box 846
Lawrence, Kansas 66044

Visit us on the World-Wide Web at www.ammpublishing.com

Copyright © 2005, Aamir M. Muhammad

All Rights Reserved. No part of this publication may be reproduced or transmitted in any form or by any means, electronic or mechanical, including photocopy, or in any other information storage and retrieval system without the expressed written permission from the author.

ISBN: 0-9754847-0-2

Library of Congress Control Number: 2004093688

Printed in Liberty, Missouri at Harmony Printing 64068
0 9 8 7 6 5 4 3 2 1

Quotations that are not attributed, are by Aamir M. Muhammad.

Warning – Disclaimer
This book is a general-purpose guide written to educate and entertain. The author, Aamir M. Muhammad, and AMM Publishing Company shall have neither liability nor responsibility to any person or entity with respect to any loss or damage caused, or alleged to have been caused to any person, directly or indirectly, by the information contained in this book.

This book may also contain errors or mistakes, and the information is only reliable for accuracy up to the date of publication, and therefore should not be considered an ultimate authority.

If you do not accept to be bound by the above statements, return this book for a full refund.

Dedication

This volume is dedicated, with praise and in humble gratitude:

To the Creator of the human mind, all systems of knowledge, and "The Word" — the Blessed Word that He has bestowed upon mankind. "In the Beginning was the Word."

To my mother, in reverence of the womb that bore me, for being my first teacher and from early childhood directing me to use my dictionary.

To my father for being my personal example of graduated growth from bottom to top, for his life of intellectual discipline, and for instilling within me a strict determination to develop creativity and make constructive contributions beyond self.

To Paulette Elizabeth Johnson-Smith who, with love and patience, taught me to read correctly.

To Imam W. Deen Mohammed for inspiring my commitment to lifelong learning; for his example of growth to spiritual and intellectual excellence, and for firmly establishing in my body of understanding that the potential for human excellence is open to every member of the human family.

To all who taught me in life, formally and informally, academically and experientially.

To Adam, mankind's first father, for correcting himself and opening the road home.

> "Nothing can stop the man with the right mental attitude from achieving his goal; nothing on earth can help the man with the wrong mental attitude."
>
> — Thomas Jefferson

Acknowledgments

Nothing ever done in life has been without the help, assistance, guidance, and encouragement of others and this book is no exception to that reality. The entire manuscript could have been one big thank you, listing an unending group of contributors that have aided me along the way and led me to write this book. Therefore, to all those contributors whose names are not listed, thank you.

Several times in my life women and men of profound character and accomplishment allowed me to walk beside them for part of their journey. They mentored me and I thank them all, now it has become my turn to mentor others. The inspiration gained from watching those who have allowed me to mentor them as they mature, accept difficult challenges and confront the fear of criticism, became fuel for writing this book. Thank you to each one of them.

The entire staff of Harmony Printing provided exceptional assistance to me, however very special thanks goes to Aimee Dennis, who applied her genius to my rough draft and vision for the book covers and transformed them into a work of art, and for her many other creative efforts to this book. Tildon Burns, for making me feel that my project was his own, and wanting for it nothing but the best each step of the way. Jeanette Marfield for being the glue that kept everyone together. If you ever decide to have a book printed, call the fine folks at Harmony Printing. (816-781-1155).

Ralph Metcalfe Jr. and Margaret Kelly provided cogent and valuable advice. Daryl Harris for creation of our beginning website design. Brian Sweeney for creation of the exhibit illustrations (artmakesme@yahoo.com). Word Co

Index Services for preparation of the index. (860-886-2532). Alan Gadney and Carolyn Porter: One-On-One Book Design & Marketing in West Hills, California for our page designs and typesetting (818-340-6620). Photographs by Chantal Caldwell of Zercher's Camera America, Lawrence, Kansas. (785-841-7205).

My friend Dave Snider, the first to answer my call for help, and Diane Greene, Tim Dismond, Damon Canada, Douglas Dahms, C. L. Wallace, Dan Williams, Terry Jacobs, Kathleen O. Smith, Alex Harris, and Mike Smith. My family members are the wings on which I've continually flown: Margaret Sharpe, Henry and Joan Jenkins, and Sandy Bryant Good.

For service above and beyond the call, thank you my brother Brian C. Jordan, for countless exceptional lessons on the meaning of the word friend.

Table of Contents

Dedication	iii
Acknowledgments	v
My Living Prayers	viii
About the Author	ix
Preface	xiii
Introduction	xv
Chapter 1 – Mental Preparation – *Comfort with Your Learning Nature*	1
Chapter 2 – The Dictionary – *Building The Foundation of a Mental Miracle*	11
Chapter 3 – Advanced Learning Method	43
Chapter 4 – Make Mathematics Easy	57
Chapter 5 – Road Map to Your Own Personal Genius	65
Afterword	71
Appendix	73
Year 2005 – 2006 Research Project Opportunity for Teachers	73
Word UP Program™	74
Professional Services	75
Scholarship Program	76
Index	77
Order Form	84

My Living Prayers

O My Beloved Children

Tasha Marie
Monique Michele
Jamar Richard
Wafa Dawn
Martha Ann

O My Beloved Grandchildren

Tiana Michele
Rae'kwon Lamont
Makayla Ann
Nashila Raquel

It has been my humbling privilege to climb upon the shoulders of those that came before me to witness lofty deeds of earthy souls and to learn from men and women of world renown, to travel this earth to 18 distant lands, all for the purpose of seeking the straight path. May you climb upon my shoulders and see the straight course and the great distance that remains beyond that which is for me to see, that you may spread the wings of your minds and souls to rise in faithful service to all mankind. Find some need and fulfill it. Find a wrong and correct it. The lasting values that transcend this world are your good deeds; therefore work hard and make them all the best. Then you will return the best of my deeds many times over.

~ Aamir M. Muhammad
2004

About the Author

While performing a third grade homework assignment to create and write several sentences for new words that had been taught in school, Aamir M. Muhammad requested from his mother the spelling of a word he wanted to use in one of the sentences he had created. His mother refused to spell the word for him and directed him to his dictionary to look up the word. Out of frustration with her response, Aamir asked his Mother: "How am I going to lookup the word in the dictionary when I don't know how to spell it?" Again his mother responded with a firm tone of voice: "Get the dictionary and figure it out." Following his Mothers orders, and yet not knowing the correct spelling, Aamir began reading the definitions of many words that were spelled similarly to his idea of the spelling for the word he was seeking.

While searching for the exact word he was after, Aamir became fascinated with all the new words he was discovering and that experience sparked his lifelong love of words and laid the foundation he would use to educate himself later in life.

During his middle and high school years Aamir's grade average remained constantly below average (D+ to C–). Several of his teachers in high school told him directly that he was "not cut out for academic studies, and would never amount to anything in life where brainpower was a requirement." Inspired by his maternal grandparent's love for, and highly refined intuitive knowledge of horticulture and agriculture, Aamir applied for admittance to the Philadelphia High School of Agriculture and Horticulture. To his amazement he was accepted. He continued his poor academic performance, however when it came to the subject of horticulture he considered himself a "see" student, if he could see it, he would learn it, and what he learned most was the science of growth.

His continuing academic frustrations and other extenuating circumstances caused him to quit high school after completing the eleventh grade. Married at the age of nineteen, he and his wife began attending weekly Bible Studies where he was chosen to read sections from Bible-related study books, an act performed before the entire group. Aamir was brought to tears and shame due to his poor reading and comprehension skills.

Understanding his dilemma, his wife advanced his reading ability by writing in his Bible Study book the phonic syllabication of every word that had three or more syllables. Armed with a new confidence in his learning ability, Aamir reached back and picked up the tool his mother had earlier provided (The Dictionary). He embarked upon a book reading binge, reading up to 25 books a month, and began the development of what is now ***The Miracle Learning System!***™.

Aamir M. Muhammad then began what has remained a lifetime commitment to education. He enrolled in the Entrepreneurial Development Training Center in Philadelphia founded by the late Rev. Dr. Leon Sullivan, majored in Business Management and graduated first in his class.

Aamir M. Muhammad's highly accomplished business career evolved, as did most pursuits in his life: starting at the bottom and working his way to the top. He worked in his uncle's New York City-based clothing and merchandising business, then moved to Ohio were he became a salesman for a local food processing company, and within an 18 month period he was promoted to Vice President for Sales and Marketing and expanded the company's product sales and distribution from one to seven states within the supermarket chain store industry. He then served as Director of Marketing for The Honorable Elijah Muhammad Memorial Health Facilities Corporation in Chicago.

During his tenure in corporate America's Fortune 500 Companies, Aamir worked in Executive Development for the National Tea Company, became the first African-American National Accounts Sales Representative for The Composite Can Group of Boise Cascade, and served as a contract consultant to Sprint and the Level 3 Communications Corporation.

Aamir's entrepreneurial development skills allowed him to create an international leather goods import company, and on a borrowed $500. investment, founded and built a national multimillion-dollar construction building materials supply company, founded and serve as CEO of a nationally-operated utilities auditing company, and built a national telecommunications real estate services company.

His civic and social responsibilities have included: service on the Board of Directors of the Cincinnati Small Business Economic Development Council; Chairman of the Board of Directors of MO-KAN National Small and Minority Contractors Association; founder and Chairman of the Board of Governors of the African-American Horticultural Society; and co-founder and National President of the National Association of Construction Contractors Cooperation.

Aamir M. Muhammad has maintained a high-octane life of growth and self-development on a horizontal rather then vertical course. His patriotic service within the American political process has included: Campaign Manager for U.S. Congressional Races in the First District of Illinois, and Third District of Kansas. He served as the Administrative Assistant to the first African-American Speaker Pro Tem of the Missouri House of Representatives.

U.S. Senate Majority Leader Bill Frist placed Aamir's name in nomination for the Senatorial Medal Of Freedom, and in year 2002 he became recipient of that award.

The Senatorial Medal of Freedom is the highest civilian honor that can be bestowed by members of the Senate. Past recipients include former President Ronald Reagan, former British Prime Minister Margaret Thatcher and Retired General Norman Schwarzkopf.

Aamir M. Muhammad, with the assistance of *The Miracle Learning System!*™, has built a life of contribution and accomplishment.

Preface

Welcome. You are about to be guided through one of the greatest methods known to man for the construction of human power: learning and mastering words. Be warned! Like many small packages, this book is extremely powerful; it will force you to ponder and think. Often you'll find yourself reading a paragraph, or just one sentence, and be forced to stop and ponder the deeper implications. Gems of learning wisdom have been sprinkled in concentrated form throughout, and they require your reflection upon them.

This book has been thoughtfully written and arranged, and it is not a feel good learning placebo; rather it is filled with interactive work assignments requiring that you read with constant location stops to perform the required assignments. Approach reading this book with the full expectation that it shall be different, even a little awkward at first; remember that you're being guided through a new and different approach to learning. This book is a roadmap, therefore read it that way, and follow its logic.

When you do the work, you get the results. Building logic is provided, however personal assembly is required. There is no magic pill that when swallowed transforms us into instant mental giants, and there are no short cuts to completing the work. This book cannot do your work for you, only you can. Summon the desire to sincerely fall in love with the learning of words.

Chapters 1 and 2 guide you through each step of this beginning journey by providing valuable keys that unlock doors for learning growth. However Chapters 3 and 4 only point you toward the precise pathways, explain what you'll find along the way, and then require you to take those keys and search for new doors to unlock on your own.

Don't Loose Your Keys!

"Words are real living miracles. When you work with words, the words work with you. When you work on words, the words work on you. When you embrace words, you and words become one."

Introduction

There are many effective ways to approach learning and *The Miracle Learning System!*™ is one of those ways. This book can help you change and improve your life. *The Miracle Learning System!*™ is about your working with words while they work on you. It is about words, and capturing their power to produce mental miracles. It is about embracing the transforming power of words and having that transforming power act upon your mind as rain falling upon a dry, desolate, and barren desert. The rain brings forth new life to the desert, and creates an oasis of rich vegetation. Words bring forth new life to your mind, and create rich intellect.

The Miracle Learning System!™ is about walking the path to the door of your own personal genius, knocking on that door and then stepping through it.

This book is not a replacement for formal academic instruction, nor should the reader assume that applying the methods taught in this book qualifies them in the very real world of academic credentials. This book does not begin to replace the immeasurable benefits obtained within institutions of higher learning; rather *The Miracle Learning System!*™ seeks among its many objectives, to assist those who for many reasons were unable to advance through those levels of instruction, and to help them build a solid foundation of confidence about their learning abilities that ultimately can lead them back to effective competition in any intellectual environment. We also seek to build higher levels of confidence within younger at-risk students who seek a different approach to shore up their mental abilities so as not to lose out on their dream of advancement to higher education.

The Miracle Learning System

History is replete with great contributors who performed poorly in school yet continued in their determination to learn how to learn and achieved intellectual excellence. *The Miracle Learning System!*™ is a celebration of learning in that spirit, and it is about learning how to learn any subject starting with the foundation of learning words. It is about the observation and demonstration of a mental miracle, and that miracle is you.

Far too many people today really believe deep down inside themselves that they are not capable of learning. Don't become one of them; do not allow yourself to believe that you do not have what it takes to learn. You do have what it takes, and the simple methods we teach you to perform in this book shall have you prove that fact to yourself. *The Miracle Learning System!*™ is about your mental worth, and overcoming the obstacles that may have been the cause of learning failures. In the universe of learning, one size does not fit all. Nothing seen in creation is growing at the same exact rate as everything else. Human minds also vary in rate of growth and learning patterns, but that does not mean that people with different growth patterns are restricted from achieving development into mental excellence.

The Miracle Learning System!™ works, it has been developed over the course of my entire life in struggle and determination to overcome my own learning deficiencies, and because of the benefits realized by me personally, my own children were taught those parts of the system that were developed during their formative years. My first-born child graduated from Langston University in Oklahoma with a degree in Early Childhood Education, and has developed early childhood education curricula for more than ten years. This is what she had to say after reading *The Miracle Learning System!*™:

Introduction

*"**The Miracle Learning System!**™ in this completed form would have greatly aided me during my college years, and would be helpful to anyone entering into higher education. Why didn't you complete this book sooner, Daddy?"*

    Tasha Muhammad — Director School Age Programs, Cincinnati, Ohio YMCA

I taught *The Miracle Learning System!*™ to many small construction contractors in concert with my entrepreneurial development courses. Many of those contractors, male and female alike, have told me that learning the performance of their skilled trades area was easy, however learning how to learn academically was a problem for them. They often expressed that their learning focus was on the skilled trade and they didn't realize how important knowing how to learn other subjects would become until they started their own businesses. In the management of their business those small contractors are finding out that their bottom line is affected by their lack of knowledge of emerging technologies and newly developed business systems and applications. They like most of us are beginning to understand that we must learn throughout our entire lifetime.

Learning is a lifelong commitment. It does not begin or end in schools, nor does it end at any age in life. Learning is a habit; there are good habits and there are bad ones that make life far more difficult than required.

Our aim here is to develop good habits in your daily learning performance. One purpose of *The Miracle Learning System!*™ is to have you, the reader, understand the processes that lead to learning growth, and become armed with the tools and knowledge that ensure that you can, in graduated steps, learn any subject you choose. *The Miracle Learning System!*™ will assist you in producing your own personal mental miracle. It takes work and dedication, however the results are worth every second of time you spend in earnest, and you shall be able to measure your progress.

You will also be automatically enrolled within a university. There are two universities that are open to just about everybody, the Universities of YKT and YDRT. Neither university requires an entrance exam, nor are tuition fees charged. Both of these universities are open all day and all night, and you can learn any subjects you choose. Best of all, the hours are flexible to meet whatever time allotment you have to devote to your educational pursuits. The Universities of Your Kitchen Table and Your Dining Room Table boast alumni rosters that list many of the best minds the world has ever encountered, and your name can be placed right along with them.

The Miracle Learning System!™ is about you and your future, and about the value we hold for your mind and its complete development. Life requires that we learn and that we comprehend the lessons it teaches us daily; thus we need to have a variety of learning tools at our disposal.

The greater the number and types of tools a construction contractor has in their tool room, the greater the ease in the performance of their skills. *The Miracle Learning System!*™ is a tool kit full of wonderful learning tools on how to learn. We are confident they can assist you throughout your entire lifetime. You can refer to this book many times over for years to come to refresh your learning skills.

Introduction

Everyone can find value with some part of this learning system, there are however several specific groups of people that this learning system should greatly benefit.

Employers should find great value in providing *The Miracle Learning System!*™ to their employees. Small, medium, and large companies alike spend vast amounts of money training and retraining their employees, many of whom have not learned how to learn.

> *"American corporations large and small should consider* **The Miracle Learning System!**™ *the new starting point in training new employees. This book should be mandatory Reading."*
>
> Brian C. Jordan, Esq. — Director, Enterprise Property Services, Sprint Corporation, Overland Park, Kansas

Students of English as a second language should also benefit greatly from this book. Using and understanding the dictionary as a foundation tool for mastering words in the English language, and building upon that foundation with a concise understanding of the tools we provide for advanced learning, will accelerate the broad comprehension requirements of English for those students.

The Miracle Learning System!™ can also aid those who have completed a horizontal rather than a vertical approach to their education. This book can help you help yourself. You only need patience and a determined desire to learn and improve.

Now Let's Begin
Your Own Personal
Mental Miracle!

> "Words are real living miracles. When you work with words, the words work with you. When you work on words, the words work on you. When you embrace words, you and words become one."

1
Mental Preparation
Comfort with Your Learning Nature

The study of horticulture and agriculture taught me the science of growth. Over the years, I began to apply principles of growth found in horticulture to other venues that developed in my life. The earth and the human mind have many similar growth principles. To achieve growth from the earth, one must prepare the earth for planting. Likewise the mind must be prepared before proper growth can occur. The first requirement in preparing the earth for new growth is to clear away and discard old, non-useful growth. Many of the notions and attitudes held in our minds related to learning are in the way and must be removed. However, removal alone is not enough. As with the earth, new and unwanted growth will quickly reappear, as do old attitudes, exactly where you are about to cultivate.

Development of a new mental attitude is the best safeguard against new unwanted growth in the fields of the mind. Understanding and acceptance of the realities regarding how the mind learns are prerequisite to forming new attitudes toward learning. When one first looks out over a field upon which one intends to cultivate for new growth, sobering realities become clear: There is a lot of work ahead. The view we have toward work is a critical issue and we must adopt the right mental attitude and the best emotional feelings with regard to work. Growth requires that first facts must be faced and the first fact that you are facing is work. Understand that the word "work" is a very good word. You must allow your inner spirit to rejoice in that word. The word "work" should no longer be associated with negative thoughts and feelings in your mind, nor in your spirit. Realize that you are now working for yourself. Starting now, work means happy! Hearing the word "work" brings inner joy and excitement.

The second procedure for development of a new attitude is to place safeguards on our ears. The structural integrity of our attitude can become subliminally damaged from simple expressions made by others, especially in those instances when we do not use our conscious mind to think about what is being said or the meaning underlining many expressions. Simple phrases said in humor and many popular catchy remarks are often filled with powerful attitude destroyers.

Do not allow yourself to automatically accept quickly spoken phrases. Examine in your mind everything you hear, and reject those expressions that conflict with the new attitude for learning that you are now developing.

With our new attitude safeguards on the ready, let's start clearing away that old unusable growth. During one of his televised speeches, former President Ronald Reagan said, "facts are stubborn objects." When you have enough of them staring you in the face, they force you to deal with them.

Fact Number One:
Learning is not hard, learning is just work.

Life requires that we bring forth a constructive fight, a positive struggle for success. Learning has the same requirement. *Get comfortable with that concept.*

Fact Number Two:
First introductions are usually awkward, and then improve.

Become comfortable within yourself with each new learning situation, and accept the fact that you don't know a thing when first introduced to a new subject. That's the way it is supposed to be, but also *accept that not knowing the subject does not mean that you won't know it.* New learning experiences are nothing more than a new adventure. Start with courage when facing anything new. Then, with time, what was new becomes an old friend.

Fact Number Three:
The human mind learns from repetition.

Expect to repeat often; don't think negative about yourself because you repeat while in the learning mode. Relax, that is the natural process. Learning is only accomplished with constant repetition. Near perfect onstage performance is the result of hours upon hours of unseen and repetitious backstage rehearsals. *Make yourself constantly want to repeat, and repeat while learning.*

Fact Number Four:
Thoughts are real things. They grow too.

Negative mental thoughts tend to run in gangs; however only one speaks first, and when a strong positive shows up then all the negatives run away. When there is no positive to be found, the whole gang of negatives attack. How you think when you're introduced to a new learning situation is critical to your learning outcome. *Think Positive.*

Fact Number Five:
What you say is exactly what you get.

During your introduction to a new learning situation, what you say aloud to yourself and to others regarding your feelings about the new learning situation generally equals your effort and learning outcome. *Always take the time to make personal attitude corrections just prior to the start of all learning situations.*

Fact Number Six:
Humans learn only through the use of one or more of the five senses.

During every learning situation in life, seek where possible to *utilize as many of your five senses as you can to accomplish your learning task.*

Fact Number Seven:
The cause of potential not reaching actual is generally effort.

When you get enough of that stuff on your side, wow, you can beat almost anything. So the question here is, *how much effort do you bring to learning?*

Fact Number Eight:
In the distance race of learning, by heart beats by memory.

When you apply all of your senses, all of your mental faculties, all of your emotions, and all of your concern to learning a subject, you are in fact learning by heart. Some call it *"knocking on the door of genius."*

Cultivation of the Mind

Once our mental field is cleared, the pulse quickens and excitement starts to build as we get closer to the planting stage, however our next step is to plow.

Several wonderful things take place in the plowing process. First the hard earth is turned and softened, next fertilizer is applied to enrich the earth, and then it is tilled to break down large chunks while mixing in the enriching fertilizer. The most essential task within that process is organizing the field in rows to prepare the earth to receive seeds of new life. New seeds of learning can never be cultivated in an unorganized mind because cluttered minds don't think right. Large volumes of new information can never be found within a thoroughly disorganized storage facility; the thinking process is retarded and inefficient and too much time is wasted trying to sort things out.

The following daily exercises will plow, fertilize, till, and organize your thinking process. These exercises will aid you in thinking right. They are simple, yet they encapsulate several profound learning mechanisms that convert your actions and thought process into automatic responses.

Each exercise utilizes some activity or function you perform every day. They will work to better anyone's situation, however these daily exercises are ideal to teach young children and start them out early on the path of organized thinking. Each daily exercise uses physical action, verbal affirmation, and daily repetition. Combining those three functions produces a powerful force to retrain the inner self.

Daily Exercise 1
Closets – Clothes – Shoes – Drawers

Closets are like minds; they are places most people outside of your personally controlled environment never get into. Start with the closets under your personal control. Just about every day that you are home you enter, acquire, exit, re-enter, deposit, and again exit one or more of your closets. They are an excellent training ground for organized thinking coupled with deliberate organized actions.

Thus your first assignment is to organize your own personal closets.

As you begin and throughout the process of establishing an organized structure in your closets, verbally repeat the following affirmation:

> Keeping an *Organized Closet* Produces an *Organized Mind*

The objective is not to just organize them once, but rather to keep them maintained daily in an organized fashion. Verbally repeat the affirmation each time you enter your closets to acquire an item. Begin the organization of the clothes in your closets by separating them into seasons—all winter/fall wear grouped together, and all summer/spring wear grouped together. Next separate the seasonal groupings by category of wear—causal, dress, business, work, etc. Divide each category into types—pants, shirts, suits, jackets, blouses, dresses, etc. Separate each type by color, then separate each color by material—cottons, silks etc. You do not have to follow this exact pattern within your own closets, however the point should be clear that your closets must become completely organized to the degree of your choosing. Shoes should also be placed in strategic order based on season, category, type, color, and all facing the same direction—all toes in, or all toes out.

Each time you enter your closets to deposit an item, verbally repeat the affirmation:

> **My Mind is *Clearly Organized***

Now apply the same logic to all your drawers. The objective is that there is a place for everything, and everything remains in its place. After you complete the task of organizing your closets, clothes, shoes, and drawers, perform the affirmations daily for ninety (90) days, remaining strict in maintaining the order you've created. After ninety days, you will find it almost impossible to return to disorganization in your thinking and actions.

Daily Exercise 2
Dress Right

The simple act of getting dressed each day is full of opportunities to retrain one's self. The daily requirement of getting dressed grants us easy access to engage the three previously discussed functions that become a powerful retraining force: physical action, verbal affirmation, and daily repetition.

Training the self to think right carries over to learning right. The mind becomes a major supporter for the establishment of right actions in all endeavors. The simple exercise we are about to describe begins a process that generates rational faith in your mind, which then allows automatic acceptance that first-thought thinking and actions are going to be right. Faculties of the heart—impulses, sentiments and feelings—begin to work harmoniously with the faculties of the mind—logic, reasoning and judgment—in the establishment of right action in all endeavors. Each time you put on your socks and shoes, always start with the right sock first, and always put on the right shoe first. While putting on the right sock, repetitiously express the following affirmation:

> **My Highest Desire is to Always *Do Right First***

While putting on the right shoe, repetitiously express the affirmation:

> *Be Right First*

Parents of young children who are still dressing them each day should say those affirmations to your child as you place their right sock and shoe on each day. Once they begin to dress themselves, instruct them on saying those affirmations on their own. The rewards for them and you shall be outstanding during their developmental years and provide lifelong benefits as well.

> *"After my introduction to the* **Miracle Learning System!**™ *I was so excited thinking about the effects it could have on my children that I couldn't wait to get home and begin teaching the system to them, and that's exactly what I did."*
>
> Damon Canada — Canada Construction, LLC
> Kansas City, Missouri

Daily Exercise 3
Applied Self Determination

Exercises 3, 4, and beyond shall be your own creation. The key for retraining the self has been given to you.

Each person is different in his or her current personal situation. Take stock of yourself; look at your habits, your attitudes, and your behavior patterns. List in honesty those negative qualities you should change, or that you know need improvement.

There is far more to getting dressed each day than putting on your socks and shoes, so use that daily repetition with other clothing items you dress into, and apply the verbal affirmations you create to improve the self. Work from the list you made of negative qualities and needed improvements, with no less then ninety days of consistency for each item. Commit to improvement of the self over your entire lifetime. Remember when creating your own exercises that each exercise incorporates the use of physical action, verbal affirmation, and daily repetition. Combining those three functions produces a powerful force to retrain the self.

Our mental field is now prepared for planting. Wow! The fun part begins, excitement is really starting to build and we can mentally visualize the new growth even before we plant the first seed.

> *"Words are real living miracles. When you work with words, the words work with you. When you work on words, the words work on you. When you embrace words, you and words become one."*

2

The Dictionary

Building the Foundation of a Mental Miracle

Continuing with the principles of growth found in the study of horticulture and agriculture, let's examine the next stages in our cultivation of new mental life with focus on some of the processes that occur and apply those realities to achieving a better understanding of our learning nature. The rudiments of planting seeds in earth require that the seeds be covered completely with earth and shielded from the light of the sun for the process of germination to take place. During the germination period, to the visible eye nothing is growing, yet there is much going on that we just can't see. After germination is completed, the seedling begins a period of great struggle, fighting its way up and breaking through the hard earth in which it is imprisoned. The seedling inherently knows that it must reach sunlight to achieve faster and sustained growth to maturity, so it endures the hardships of that struggle until it succeeds.

Once the seedling reaches the bright light of the sun, the water within it is converted by that sunlight into a dynamic fuel. Then with our own human eyes we can see that seedling start to grow at an awesome rate. That process of transformation of a tiny seed is such a wonderful miracle to watch unfold that it has amazed me all my life. The fields of our human minds are very similar to the earth, as are the rudimentary processes that take place in our learning mode. New words are new seeds, and while at first introduction to their use and potential they seem awkward to us, still we receive them, and bury them into our mind. Once we begin to work with that new word, it germinates, and we struggle with its uses and applications until that new word reaches up to meet our rational understanding of its full context. That process causes an explosion in our intellect, and phenomenal mental growth begins. Words are our key to beginning mental and intellectual expansion, so we shall begin our learning miracle within the home man has made for words—the dictionary.

It really is worth your time to read the dictionary, including that part of the dictionary we so often pass up—the beginning section, which explains how the dictionary works. The "elements" of the dictionary provide marvelous insight into the ways words are displayed for our learning convenience. One of my dictionaries lists over thirty different elements that relate to every word in the dictionary. There is a wonderful education waiting for you within the first few pages of your dictionary.

The Best Investment

The Universities of YKT and YDRT do not require you to pay tuition, however you must provide your own books. The first required book is a dictionary, and my suggestion is that you make a real investment and acquire the very best two that your financial situation allows. Why purchase two dictionaries, why not just one? When you examine dictionaries you will quickly find that none are exactly alike. Each contains different variations of word definitions and words may be found in one that can't be found in another. Owning a very high quality pair of dictionaries can be an enriching experience. The most important reason to invest in a couple of really good dictionaries is that you're going to be spending a lot of time in them, specifically for the next year, and hopefully for the remainder of your life.

The reading exercises taught in this chapter yield introduction to many new seeds or words that you will plant in your mental field. You're going to struggle, and that is expected. Remember to remain calm and confident. Soon you are going to be able to measure your success and further increase your learning confidence. The dictionary you purchase is the tool used to advance your intellectual growth at super rates of speed, but things will take their natural course and the beginning shall be as it should be—slow.

Preliminary Dictionary Reading

Read all the beginning sections in your dictionary, the sections that come before the alphabetical listing of words. The purpose is just to familiarize you with the material presented in these sections. Don't try to memorize them, just read each word of each section in the beginning of your dictionary, and become acquainted with the information.

Don't worry about the words that you do not know during your first reading of the beginning sections of your dictionary. You'll soon return there to perform a preliminary informal reading exercise applying the methods outlined below. Pay attention to the sections on pronunciation, usage and the elements of the dictionary. After you reach your comfort zone with these exercises, and you will, you shall find that on your own accord you will often refer to those sections for continued reinforcement from the instruction they provide.

Required Materials

In order to perform the following five Formal Reading Exercises, you will need to purchase or have available five different colored highlighter markers. The colors you should use are yellow, green, orange, red and blue. Additionally you need to have three legal pads devoted strictly to these exercises, and several scratch pads. Use additional pads as needed to complete each exercise. You will need your dictionary, and a pen or pencil, and you must keep a watch or clock near you every time you have a reading period.

Now pick a subject that you know you don't know, and do not pick an easy subject. It will be helpful to you to pick a subject in which you have some interest, or have wanted to learn for some time but never attempted to learn. Now this part is very important—buy a book on that subject. You must own the book because you are going to mark up the book a lot. Do not use a library book or any book that is not your own personal property.

Required Materials Check List

- ✔ two (2) high quality dictionaries
- ✔ a book on the subject you want to learn
- ✔ five (5) different color highlighter markers
- ✔ three (3) legal pads
- ✔ clock or wristwatch
- ✔ pens or pencils
- ✔ scratch pads

General Performance for Each Formal Reading Exercise

Use the book you purchase on the subject matter you chose to learn continuously throughout each Formal Reading Exercise of which there are five, divided into Reading Periods.

A Formal Reading Exercise consists of reading your entire subject book one time, cover to cover complete. *The Miracle Learning System!*™ requires you to read your subject book five separate times, each divided into Reading Periods of varying amounts of time. The amount of time you spend reading, and the amount of material you read during each Reading Period is based on the time you have to devote to any Reading Period. Just as those time amounts will vary, so shall the amount of material you read. Learning how to learn really starts now. You will learn how to measure your learning progress with each Formal Reading Exercise.

Performance Instructions

NOTE! Do not begin performance of your first Formal Reading Exercise after reading these performance instructions. The following instructions are to acquaint you with the entire process of a Formal Reading Exercise and to prepare you for performance of two informal reading exercises. For your reference we provide you here with the instructions for Formal Reading Exercise 1.

Formal Reading Exercise 1

Read the entire book, divided into Reading Periods. Devote whatever time you have allotted to read in the comfort of your home, and when you have completed a Reading Period, use a bookmark to mark that spot in your book, so that you can continue your next Reading Period exactly where you left off. Speed is not a factor in this learning experience, so do not be concerned with how much time you do or don't have to spend during any Reading Period. Focus on being consistent in your effort and completing the entire process regardless of the time it takes.

At the very top on the first sheet of one of your legal pads, write down the words "Exercise 1—Minutes Spent During Each Reading Period." Number each line down the left side on that same sheet of legal paper, i.e., 1, 2, 3, 4, etc. Each line represents a complete Reading Period. Divide the paper into three equal sized vertical columns, and write the following three subheadings just above line 1:

1. Start Time
2. Finish Time
3. Total Time This Reading Period

Whenever you begin a Reading Period mark down the time when you start reading. When you finish that same Reading Period, mark down on the same line the time when you stopped reading. Subtract the time you started from the time you stopped, and write down on that same line the total minutes spent during that Reading Period (see Example 1). Continue writing the minutes down for each Reading Period on each successive line, and on however many pages of your legal pad needed until you complete Exercise 1. We will explain later the reason behind that action. You will continue to use that same legal pad throughout your performance of all five Formal Reading Exercises.

	EXERCISE #1 MINUTES SPENT DURING EACH READING PERIOD		
	START TIME	FINISH TIME	TOTAL TIME THIS READING PERIOD
1	6:00	6:45	45 MIN
2	6:45	7:45	1 HOUR
3	6:00	7:00	1 HOUR
4	6:15	7:00	45 MIN
5	6:15	7:15	1 HOUR
6			
7			

Example 1

Do not write the dates for each Reading Period, we are not concerned with time in that context. It does not matter if you take one week, one month, or however long to complete Formal Reading Exercise 1. Finally, to clear away any confusion—a Reading Exercise is the completed reading of the entire subject book. A Reading Period is the number of minutes that you spend reading each time you read the subject book.

The heart of *The Miracle Learning System!*™ dwells in Formal Reading Exercise 1. This exercise will take far longer than the next four Formal Reading Exercises to perform. Do not become discouraged or impatient with yourself. There is more benefit than you realize mounting up in your favor as you complete the entire process. Endure beginning frustrations and just complete the exercise. At the conclusion of Formal Reading Exercise 2 you will be amazed, and proud that you stayed the course.

Read the entire book on the subject matter you have chosen to learn. Read every word of every page in the book. Do not attempt to read fast. Divide the reading of the entire book into as many Reading Periods as you require. Keep a record of the minutes spent reading during each reading period.

During each reading period, use the yellow highlighter marker, and draw a yellow highlighted line through each word in your subject book for which you do not know the following: (See Example 1-A)

- ✔ The correct pronunciation.
- ✔ The definition, or word meaning.
- ✔ How to spell the word.

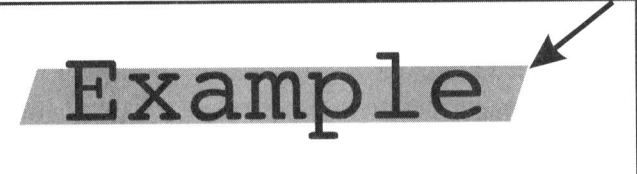

Example 1-A

Each time you encounter a word about which you do not know one or more of the above, immediately stop reading and look the word up in your dictionary.

Focus on pronunciation first. Remember to consult the elements section of the dictionary to assist you with the rules of pronunciation. While reviewing the elements section, give your attention to the pronunciation key—primary stress, secondary stress, syllabication dots and the verbal illustration. Then go back to the word you looked up and practice saying the word over and over five times using the guidance provided in the elements section of your dictionary. The first several words that you engage in this process will yield slow and awkward progress toward your comfort zone. Trust yourself, and keep working with the word and its pronunciation. After the first few words, you will gain greater comfort with learning correct pronunciation.

Next focus on learning the word's meaning or definition; read the meaning slowly five times. When necessary, refer to the usage notes in the front sections of your dictionary to better understand the "context" in which the word is used in every day speech. In your head, make up three different sentences using the word. Now pronounce the word correctly again and, without reading the dictionary, say the definition of the word out loud from memory. If you're still not confident that you now know the word by heart, repeat reading the pronunciation and definition of the word until you are confident that you have mastered that word.

Remember that learning is caused by repetition.

Now learn to spell the word by reading the correct word spelling from the dictionary, and saying the letters as you read out loud, followed by saying the word with correct pronunciation. Do that three times.

After performing repeat reading and out loud pronunciation, close your eyes, visualize the word spelled correctly, and spell the word out loud three times with your eyes closed.

Open your eyes and repeat the word three more times, reading the correct spelling of the word from the dictionary. Say the letters out loud, followed by saying the word with correct pronunciation. Now write the word on your scratch pad, without looking at the dictionary, and then continue on with your reading of your subject book and complete your reading period.

Each time, and no matter how often you find a word that you do not know, stop and repeat the routine you just performed, starting with drawing a yellow highlighted line through the word in your subject book, and repeat those same steps again. Take your time with this process. Be consistent and complete the process for each word you do not know as you come upon them.

On the top of the first sheet of your second legal pad write the words "New Words Not Found in Dictionary in Formal Reading Exercise 1." Number each line down on the sheet of legal paper, i.e., 1, 2, 3, 4, etc. On this legal pad you will keep the number sequence continuing without interruption throughout Formal Reading Exercise 1. Write down each word that you do not find in your dictionary on that same legal pad. Continue to write down each word not found in your dictionary on a numbered line during the entire Formal Reading Exercise 1 (see Example 2).

	NEW WORDS NOT FOUND IN DICTIONARY IN FORMAL EXERCISE #1
1	ARTICULATE
2	PROPOSITION
3	COMMUNICATE
4	SUPPOSITION
5	TRANSLATE
6	
7	

Example 2

When you complete your Reading Period, count the number of words that you highlighted in yellow, and on the first sheet of your third legal pad, write down the words "Exercise 1—Number of Words Found That Were Unknown During Each Reading Period." Number each line down on the sheet of legal paper, i.e., 1, 2, 3, 4, etc. Each line represents a complete reading period. Whenever you end a reading period, mark down the total number of unknown words found during your reading period. Do not write down the words, only the total number of new words found (see Example 3).

	EXERCISE #1 NUMBER OF WORDS FOUND THAT WERE UNKNOWN DURING EACH READING PERIOD
1	4
2	1
3	0
4	2
5	0
6	
7	

Example 3

Attention!

Re-read the instructions above several times before you perform each Reading Period during Formal Reading Exercise 1. Keep your healthy new attitude for work. Completing Formal Reading Exercise 1 in its entirety will be one of the greatest gifts you have ever presented to yourself.

Performance of Two Preliminary Informal Reading Exercises

Preliminary 1

Follow all the instructions you've just read exactly, and perform your first informal reading exercise by reading the front sections of your dictionary. Mark each word you do not know in yellow and complete each of the steps as instructed on the performance for a Formal Reading Exercise.

Once you have completed your preliminary reading exercise using your dictionary's beginning sections, you shall have gained greater comfort and familiarity with the method required to complete each of the five required Formal Reading Exercises that follow.

Preliminary 2

Now begin your second informal reading exercise by bookmarking this page, and highlight the page number using your yellow highlighter. Close this book and restart your reading of this book from cover to cover using the same methods for the performance of Formal Reading Exercise 1. Master every word written in this book. *The Miracle Learning System!*™ is written at the reading grade level of 10.0. After performing both preliminary reading exercises continue on with the reading and follow the instructions below.

Review of Instructions for Formal Reading Exercise 1

Purchase:

1. two (2) high quality dictionaries
2. a book on the subject you want to learn
3. five (5) different color highlighter markers
4. three (3) legal pads
5. clock or wristwatch
6. pens or pencils
7. scratch pads

Action Items:

1. Read the beginning sections of your dictionary.
2. Read the entire book on the subject you want to learn, using Reading Periods, until the book is completed.
3. Use one legal pad to track your minutes spent during each Reading Period.
4. Use another legal pad to write each new word not found in your dictionary.

5. Use another legal pad to track the total number of new words found during each Formal Reading Period.

6. Use the yellow highlighter to draw a line through each word in your subject book that you do not know.

7. Learn to correctly pronounce each unknown word.

8. Learn the definition of each unknown word.

9. Learn to correctly spell each unknown word.

Now begin complete performance of Formal Reading Exercise 1, using the subject book you chose to learn. Then return here and continue reading.

Field Trip

Before you begin performance of Formal Reading Exercise 2, take a trip to your local library. Take with you the legal pad on which you wrote, "New Words Not Found in Dictionary in Formal Reading Exercise 1." Go to the library's reference desk and ask the librarian for a couple of quality dictionaries, and make sure that the dictionaries given to you are different from those you have at home.

Now look up each word on your list in the library's dictionaries, and follow the instructions given to you in this chapter. Most libraries have photocopy machines, and you may want to make a photocopy of the definition for each word on your list. Also take a look at the sections in the front of the dictionaries you are using at the library; maybe you'll pick up a few good instructions that are not available in the dictionaries you have at home.

After you have completed your field trip assignment, continue on with reading the instructions and perform Formal Reading Exercise 2.

Formal Reading Exercise 2

Congratulations on completing Formal Reading Exercise 1. You should be extremely proud of your accomplishment. The hardest work is getting through the first complete reading of your subject book. From here on each Formal Reading Exercise gets easier, however you must not rush any part of the process. Do the work completely, and keep your pace slow and steady. Consistency in combination with deliberate action will manifest many hidden benefits during your development. The discipline you placed upon yourself to complete Formal Reading Exercise 1 has now placed you in a very special category of people. You have also now placed the first tap on the door of your own personal genius.

Formal Reading Exercise 2 is exactly the same as Formal Reading Exercise 1 with one exception: stop using the yellow highlighter marker and replace it with the green marker.

Use of the Green Highlighter

In Formal Reading Exercise 1 you placed a yellow line through each word in your study book that you did not know, and were required to look up the definition for those words in your dictionary. In this Formal Reading Exercise, place a green vertical line through the last letter of each word for which you still find difficulty in remembering the correct pronunciation, definition and spelling (see Example 4). Be honest with yourself and mark the word if you still are having problems with it. You should not be finding new words that you don't know in this Formal Reading Exercise. The only words that should be difficult for you are some of the words already marked in yellow.

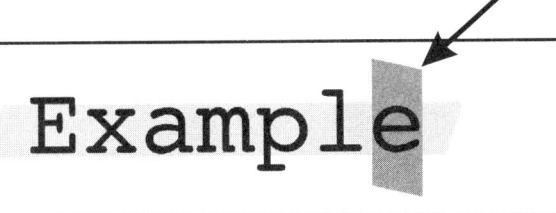

Example 4

Review of Instructions for Formal Reading Exercise 2

Action Items:

1. Stop using the yellow highlighter.

2. Start using the green highlighter and draw a vertical line through the last letter of each word that you are still having difficulty learning.

3. Re-read the entire book on the subject you want to learn, using Reading Periods, until it is completed.

4. Use a legal pad to track your minutes spent during each Reading Period.

5. Use another legal pad to track the total number of words found during each Reading Period that are still giving you difficulty in learning, those that you have placed a green vertical line through.

6. Continue to learn to correctly pronounce each word you still have difficulty with by re-looking it up and performing the same learning technique used in Formal Reading Exercise 1 to master that word.

7. Continue to learn the definition of each word with which you still have difficulty.

8. Continue to learn to correctly spell each word you still have difficulty spelling from memory.

9. Do not read fast. Because the information is more comfortable now, it is natural to try and rush your second reading of the study book, however you will miss out on valuable development if you rush.

NOTE! In this and the remaining Formal Reading Exercises, you will be using only two (2) legal pads. The need to write words not found in your dictionary should no longer exist. Use of your third legal pad will begin again when you choose to learn a new subject.

Now begin Complete Performance of Formal Reading Exercise 2. Then return here and continue reading.

Mental Elevation Marker

If you never have had the opportunity to drive up and down a mountain, know that it can be an exhilarating experience. One quickly notices that there are elevation markers posted up and down the mountain one mile apart that indicate the current height reached in miles above sea level. Also you quickly become aware of the powerful expanded range of your vision as you make your way higher. The accomplishment you have achieved in the performance of completing the first two Formal Reading Exercises is in many ways the equal to driving up a mountain. The difference is that the mountain you're ascending is a mental or intellectual mountain, and you are achieving higher mental and intellectual range. Now let's examine exactly what you have achieved thus far by completing the first two Formal Reading Exercises.

Let's start by looking at your discipline development. Just as a body builder slowly but progressively builds body muscle mass, form, and strength with consistent weight exercise; you have been building mental and intellectual discipline performing each of your Reading Periods within the past two Formal Reading Exercises. That is why we refer to each reading action as an exercise. Your mental strength is far greater now than when you first began studying *The Miracle Learning System!*™. If you also have begun to apply the exercises in Chapter 1, you have made life-altering changes to your mind and character that additionally are building and strengthening your mental discipline. There should be developing within you a noticeable change for the better in your attitude and your self-esteem, along with diminishing fears about learning. You're making serious progress, so be proud, continue to do the work and stay the course.

Another Mental Elevation Marker essential for you to look at now is the legal pad that has been tracking the total number of unknown words that you recorded in Formal Reading Exercise 1.

Whatever that total number is, it represents the total number of words now added to your vocabulary. Whether that number is only 1 or as much as 100, it represents improvement in your mental growth, expanded intellectual capacity, and greater reading comprehension skills.

Now examine the total number of words you tracked for Formal Reading Exercise 2 that you are having difficulty mastering. Deduct the number of words tracked in Formal Reading Exercise 2 from the number of words tracked in Formal Reading Exercise 1 and you have a number, regardless of size, that represents an expanded intellect. It also represents an improvement in your learning ability, and most importantly, it should provide you with increased strength to eliminate any remaining intimidation about your ability to learn. The Elevation Marker is saying, "you're making progress in the elimination of those subconscious negatives."

Formal Reading Exercise 3

Formal Reading Exercise 3 is exactly the same as Formal Reading Exercise 2 with only one exception: stop using the green highlighter marker and replace it with the orange marker.

Use of the Orange Highlighter

In Formal Reading Exercise 2 you placed a green line through the last letter of each word in your study book for which you still found difficulty in remembering the pronunciation, definition, and correct spelling, and were required to re-look up those words in your dictionary. In this Formal Reading Exercise, place an orange vertical line through the first letter of each word for which you still find difficulty in remembering the pronunciation, definition and correct spelling (see Example 5). Be honest with yourself, and mark the word if you still are having problems with it.

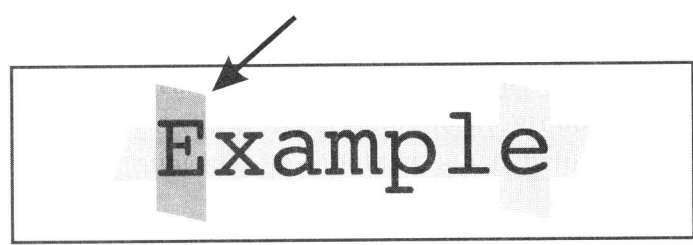

Example 5

Review of Instructions for Formal Reading Exercise 3

1. Stop using the green highlighter.

2. Start using the orange highlighter and draw a vertical line through the first letter of each word that you are still having difficulty learning.

3. Re-read the entire book on the subject you want to learn, using Reading Periods, until it is completed.

4. Use one legal pad to track your minutes spent during each Reading Period.

5. Use another legal pad to track the total number of words found during each Reading Period that are still giving you difficulty in learning, those through which you have placed a orange vertical line.

6. Continue to learn to correctly pronounce each word with which you still have difficulty by re-looking it up and performing the same learning technique used in Formal Reading Exercise 1 to master that word.

7. Continue to learn the definition of each word with which you still have difficulty.

8. Continue to learn to correctly spell each word you still have difficulty spelling from memory.

9. Do not read fast. Because the information is more comfortable now, it is natural to try and rush your third reading of the study book but you will miss out on valuable development if you rush.

Now begin Complete Performance of Formal Reading Exercise 3. Then return here and continue reading.

Levelheaded Thinking

The excitement of mental growth does strange things to some people. The advancement they acquire in life—in money, fame, or knowledge—often seduces them into arrogance, false pride, and worse. The people that are most admired tend to be those who have made great achievements while remaining levelheaded down-to-earth regulars among us commoners. The journey you're currently pursuing must be safeguarded against the subtle seduction of those negative qualities.

The mental growth that has already begun in you is only a small fraction of what is to come. Take a look at your Elevation Marker as you did after concluding Formal Reading Exercise 2. This time, pay close attention to the difference in the total number of minutes it took you to complete each of the three (3) Formal Reading Exercises thus far. With each exercise you have completed, there should be measurable progress that ought to have you feeling very good about yourself and your impending future growth. Stay levelheaded.

Formal Reading Exercise 4

Formal Reading Exercise 4 is exactly the same as Formal Reading Exercise 3 with only one exception: stop using the orange highlighter marker and replace it with the red marker.

Use of the Red Highlighter

In Formal Reading Exercise 3 you placed an orange line through each word in your study book for which you still found it difficult to remember the pronunciation, definition, correct spelling, and were required to re-look up the definition for those words in your dictionary. In this Formal Reading Exercise, place a red dot under the center of each word of which you still find it difficult to remember the pronunciation, definition and correct spelling (see Example 6). Be honest with yourself, and mark the word if you still are having problems with it. You should almost be reading the entire book with little pause to look up words in your dictionary during your reading periods. Again, we place the stress on reading slowly, it is even more important that you do so now.

Example 6

Review of Instructions for Formal Reading Exercise 4

1. Stop using the orange highlighter.

2. Start using the red highlighter and place a red dot under the center of each word that you are still having difficulty learning.

3. Re-read the entire book on the subject you want to learn, using Reading Periods, until it is completed.

4. Use one legal pad to track your minutes spent during each Reading Period.

5. Use another legal pad to track the total number of words found during each Reading Period that are still giving you difficulty in learning, those that you have placed a red dot under.

6. Continue to learn to correctly pronounce each word you still have difficulty with by re-looking it up and performing the same learning technique used in Formal Reading Exercise 1 to master it.

7. Continue to learn the definition of each word with which you still have difficulty.

8. Continue to learn to correctly spell each word you still have difficulty spelling from memory.

9. Do not read fast. Because the information is more comfortable now, it is natural to try and rush your fourth reading of the study book, however you will miss out on valuable development if you rush.

Now begin complete performance of Formal Reading Exercise 4. Then return here and continue reading.

Bedrock

There are many curriculum developers and ranking education administrators who agree that more than any other factor, reading ability is the greatest contributor to the human capacity to learn any and all subjects including math. The ability to read is the bedrock upon which learning is built. Reading ability is nothing more than one's ability to comprehend words that are presented in varying combinations in sentence and paragraph structure.

Reading comprehension is achieved when the words presented are understood in the context of how they are presented. Simply stated, the more words you know, the better your ability to learn any subject. Words are seeds for cultivation in the fields of the mind. The more seeds planted, the bigger the crop size and the greater the potential for high yield.

One of the key purposes for performing both preliminary and Formal Reading Exercises is to plant new seeds—words—in the fields of your mind, to have you know and understand them in varying contexts, and to begin to get a feel for how they can be presented.

> *"Teacher and student, mentor and protégé will find practical daily application of the tools presented within this* **Miracle Learning System!**™ *Many speak of life-long learning but they offer nothing beyond rhetoric. This system presents logical steps with identifiable metrics."*
>
> **Dan J. Williams — President and CEO, Masters, Williams and Associates, Inc., Vadnais Heights, Minnesota**

You are making great progress in that regard and yet we still are only at the bedrock, the foundation. Let's turn to the field of construction and place it along side horticulture and agriculture to extract the gems of wisdom those disciplines provide about the science of growth.

In construction, any structure has to be built in accord with the size of the foundation upon which it rests. The foundation for a house cannot support the construction of a towering skyscraper. It logically follows that one must predetermine the size of the structure they wish to build before preparing a foundation that will support the proposed structure.

In horticulture and agriculture, the next requirement for growth is to cut into and dig away the hard earth in preparation for planting, and in construction the same principle applies for the foundation to be laid. The higher up one intends for a structure to be built, the deeper down into the earth they must dig. The foundation must not only be dug deep for taller structures, it must also be broad so as to accept the weight of that structure.

Once the earthwork and foundation are complete, the structure begins to be built, one floor up at a time. Hundred-story skyscrapers go up one floor at a time. Now let's follow that logic to its natural conclusion related to our mental growth and ability to learn. Whatever level of mental growth you seek must be supported with an equal-sized vocabulary foundation, with full understanding and comprehension related to that vocabulary. The more you want to learn, the greater the size of your vocabulary requirement.

Increased vocabulary understanding must go beyond small words and expand to words of greater complexity. The mental work and struggle to master complex words and definitions is equal to digging down deep into the earth to establish the foundation necessary to support the large mental structure we seek to build. Also the requirement for our mental foundation to be broad enough to support our mental structure demands that our learning interest go beyond a few simple subjects. Thus we need to build our vocabulary with the understanding of words in a wide range of subjects. The mental growth we seek comes in stages, one level at a time.

With completion of Formal Reading Exercise 4 your ability to read and understand every single word in your study book should be nearly accomplished. When you have mastered every word in your study book of a new and difficult subject, what an outstanding accomplishment that will be for you. In the next chapter we provide you with additional tools that can advance learning of new and difficult subjects.

Formal Reading Exercise 5

Formal Reading Exercise 5 is exactly the same as Formal Reading Exercise 4 with only one exception: stop using the red highlighter marker and replace it with the blue marker.

Use of the Blue Highlighter

In Formal Reading Exercise 4 you placed a red dot under the center of each word in your study book for which you still found it difficult to remember the pronunciation, definition and correct spelling, and were required to re-look up the definition for those words in your dictionary. In this Formal Reading Exercise, place a blue dot under the center of each word, next to the last dot you made, for which you still find difficulty in remembering the correct pronunciation, definition and spelling (see Example 7).

Example 7

Do not allow the excitement of being nearly complete with all the Formal Reading Exercises force you into faster reading. The new seeds need strong roots and cultivation. Take your time, read slowly, and allow the words to work on you as you are working on the words you're reading.

Review of Instructions for Formal Reading Exercise 5

1. Stop using the red highlighter.

2. Start using the blue highlighter and place a blue dot, next to the last red dot, under the center of each word that you are still having difficulty learning.

3. Re-read the entire book on the subject you want to learn, using Reading Periods, until it is completed.

4. Use one legal pad to track your minutes spent during each Reading Period.

5. Use another legal pad to track the total number of words found during each Reading Period that are still giving you difficulty in learning, those under which you have placed a blue dot.

6. Continue to learn to correctly pronounce each word you still have difficulty with by re-looking up each word and performing the same learning technique used in Formal Reading Exercise 1 to master it.

7. Continue to learn the definition of each word with which you still have difficulty.

8. Continue to learn to correctly spell each word you still have difficulty spelling from memory.

Do not read fast.

Begin Complete Performance of Formal Reading Exercise 5. Then return here and continue reading.

Knocking on the Door of Your Personal Genius

Look at all your marvelous achievements thus far. Earlier we said that you have placed yourself in a very special category of people and you are now in the elite of that group. The discipline required to follow all the steps of the five reading exercises through to completion is an exceptional testament to your mental abilities and potential.

The action that now places you in the elite group is the fact that very few people pick up a book on a new and difficult subject and make it their purposed task to know and understand every single word in that book, and you have just done that. Count the total number of new words you've added to your vocabulary. Compare the reduction in total minutes it took for you to complete each of the five reading exercises. That reduction in minutes, when examined in percentage of reduction from one to the next reading exercise, underscores the percentage of increase in your reading comprehension. We are so proud of what you have done that if we were there, we would give you the biggest hug. So please consider yourself hugged.

Having completed five separate readings of the entire book on the new subject you chose to learn has facilitated your creation of a bedrock foundation in your knowledge and understanding regarding that subject. Your ability to now advance and build upon that knowledge is very sound. The fears you might have been harboring about learning that subject are conquered. You have truly gone from tapping to knocking on the door of your personal genius.

"Words are real living miracles. When you work with words, the words work with you. When you work on words, the words work on you. When you embrace words, you and words become one."

Proclamation

The Alumni of the
Universities of YKT and YDRT

Whereas, you adopted and implemented
the Daily Exercises as outlined in
Chapters 1 and 2 of this book,
and Whereas, you have completed all
Five Separate Readings of the entire book
on the new subject you chose to learn,
and Whereas, you have Expanded Your
Vocabulary and Reading Comprehension,

The Alumni of the Universities of YKT and YDRT
hereby confer upon you the title of Associate
and place for evermore

Your Name

Among the names of those great minds
that passed before you through
he hallowed halls of knowledge.

3
Advanced Learning Method

We continue from here to build on the foundation we have completed, using the same approach for learning: working with the word. It is essential that you understand the different approach we are taking in learning how to learn. Words are the key for building basic understanding and comprehension. The more words you understand about a subject, the greater your comprehension of that subject.

We started your learning process by focusing on building vocabulary, and with performance of two informal preliminary reading exercises and five Formal Reading Exercises with the textbook on the subject you chose to learn. That textbook reading experience was your introduction to that new subject, and only familiarized you with a foundation of general insight on the subject you chose to learn.

Several other important accomplishments were achieved in that process, however you cannot think of yourself as expert in that subject, though you know every word in your textbook. The standard approach relies on continuation with advanced textbook instruction centered on teaching the subject through solving more advanced problems associated with the subject to build one's knowledge to achieve subject mastery. Our focus remains on the word and now, the language of the words related to a subject.

> *"Truly a unique educational tool! I shall make this book available to all my employees."*
>
> Douglas M. Dahms, P.E. — Real-Estate Developer & General Contractor Arvada, Colorado

Travel to foreign countries where a different language is spoken is a very sobering experience. One quickly learns that deficient language skill becomes the primary cause of everything being limited. The ability to gain complete mobility, access, and understanding of all that the new foreign environment offers is narrowed. One remains completely dependent on others and on the knowledge limits of those upon whom they must depend. One departs that country less enriched than what was possible because they did not know the language.

New subjects are no different than visiting a new foreign land. You will accomplish far more when you know the language. The greater your understanding of the language of any new subject, the greater your ability to master learning that subject and become expert. All subjects have their own language. Words that are used in the language body of a subject often have completely different definition use in a basic dictionary of words of the English language.

The language of a subject often broadens a single word to define a concept, process or function related to that subject. Therefore *The Miracle Learning System!*™ approach teaches you to learn the language of the subjects you select as the next logical step in learning mastery.

Organized Systems of Knowledge

The accumulated body of knowledge amassed by mankind is awesome in every dimension imaginable. Every branch of the human family has acquired, advanced, and contributed to mankind's accumulated body of knowledge. The explosion of new processes and applications over the past few decades has produced an enormous amount of advanced knowledge and information. Rapidly advancing new technologies, applications and processes are just beginning to accelerate. Given that premise, our requirement to consistently learn and relearn shall only increase.

Should the premise just described be true, it places even greater emphasis on our ability to understand how organized systems of knowledge work. The same way you placed all your closets and clothing into a system, mankind has done the same with knowledge and information. It is arguably more important today to learn how and where to find the knowledge and information you seek as it is to acquire it.

The vastness of accumulated knowledge has made the keepers of the word more valuable than the keepers of the money. Before we can effectively master the language of any new subject, we must know where to find the most authoritative sources of pinpoint accurate knowledge about the language of that subject. We must also know the diverging paths and compartments within our subject language.

Organized Sources of The Word

The four advanced resource tools for learning words upon which we shall focus our attention are: Dictionaries, Glossaries of Terms, Thesauri and Encyclopedias. We must learn and thoroughly understand the vast number of different types of those resource tools that exist. We must know the context in which each is used, and how to locate them.

The greatest source of wealth in learning the mastery of words is found mostly within those advanced tools.

Each one of those resources is organized in different categories of books, and all the different types of books under that category heading divide each category. There are far more than four advanced resource tools for learning words, however our focus remains with those four named.

Dictionaries

The total number of different types of dictionaries is overwhelming. The two primary forms are basic word usage and subject word usage dictionaries.

Basic word usage dictionaries focus on general words of the English language and provide word definition and detailed information related to the pronunciation, spelling, history or etymology of words, and basic word usage. There are scores of different publishers of basic language dictionaries. Each dictionary published is different in how extensive a selection of words they display, and each provides slightly different word definitions. There are basic language dictionaries for every foreign language, and there are foreign language dictionaries that translate English into other languages, and other languages into English while still providing basic usage information for the words they translate.

The greatest proliferations of dictionaries, however, are subject dictionaries. Those are the ones that serve our purposes very well in our advanced stage of learning how to learn. Almost every subject under the sun has a dictionary wherein one finds instruction on the concise definitions of words and phrases as used strictly within that subject. Groups of categories divide subject dictionaries, which are then again divided by type. Types are then divided by specific discipline. As an example of how that system of organization works, let's examine the group of subject dictionaries on Mathematics, and a couple of the many categories within that group: Geometry and Algebra.

Let's look at just a few of the many different types of dictionaries that can be found related to each specific discipline.

Geometry Dictionaries

1. The Dictionary of Geometrical Systems

2. The Dictionary of Geometrical Symbols

3. The Dictionary of Geometry Words

4. The Dictionary of Basic Geometry Terms

Algebra Dictionaries

1. The Banach Algebra Dictionary

2. The Dictionary of Algebraic Systems

3. The Dictionary of Terms used in Algebra

In the Preface of this book we said that you would be guided each step of the way through Chapters 1 and 2 and we also told you that Chapters 3 and 4 would only point you toward the precise pathways in the advanced learning methods. What we have just explained regarding " Subject Dictionaries" adjunct what follows in this and the next chapter requires self-direction. The necessity for that requirement shall become self-evident as you research and delve deeper into each of the vast resource tools we point your attention toward.

After you complete five formal reading exercises for all future new subjects you choose to learn, you must commit yourself to do the research and find all the advanced tools available to you for mastering each Subject Language for each subject you are studying. That is your key for building your vocabulary, your reading comprehension, and your intellect to the greatest heights.

Glossaries of Terms

Most often our attention to glossaries relates to the list of words at the end of a book, an alphabetical listing of special words only found in that book. There are, however, wide varieties of glossaries that provide insight and understanding specific to the terms used in many different industries and professions.

Glossaries of professional terms are available from professional trades associations and publishers of general educational materials. Trades associations operating on behalf of any specific profession you're interested in learning are a great place to begin research for glossaries of the terms used in that area of knowledge.

The following is a very small sampling of professional glossaries of terms that are available.

1. The Glossary of Dental Terminology
2. The Glossary of Financial Terminology
3. The Glossary of Medical Terms
4. The Glossary of Insurance Terminology
5. The Glossary of Statistical Terms
6. The Glossary of Mathematical Programming
7. Mathematics Glossary
8. Actuarial Glossary

The list of professional glossaries is as long as the list of professions. The same term that may be used within one profession may also be used within a totally different profession with a completely different definition. Thus glossaries are an excellent resource for expanding one's comprehension of terms and words in multiple contexts.

Our main objective is to expand our word vocabulary upward through each layer or level of word usage in all contexts, regardless of their application in a subject or profession, or as used within a particular industry.

We want to comprehend as many uses of words, phrases, and terms as possible. We're building our mental structure as high as possible; therefore we must seek out every word tool available and work with the words to extract all the angles of meanings established with their uses.

> **Reminder:**
> *Perform the same process you completed in the five Formal Reading Exercises utilizing your selections of dictionaries and glossaries. Be patient with yourself, don't read fast, and build the strength of your memory by learning the terms, formulas, rules and phrases associated with advanced word sources.*

Thesauri

Thesauri, unlike encyclopedias, are very different in layout from that of dictionaries, and they serve a different purpose. Thesauri provide expanded word possibilities on those occasions when you know a word you want to use but it's just not the exact word you want.

Thesauri are wonderful word finders that offer a variety of alternative word choices. There are several different types of thesauri in use. One type commonly used identifies synonyms (words that are the same or nearly the same in meaning) or antonyms (words or expressions that have the opposite meaning of a given word or expression).

There are also professional or technical thesauri that place their focus on different technical and professional fields and specific fields of study. Researchers generally use those thesauri for selecting the most appropriate words and terms related to their research because they offer specialized vocabulary within their given field.

In short however, thesauri are books that show related words and connections between words. They are a great treasure trove rich with different word choices.

A thesaurus can be confusing when first becoming acquainted with its use. Just remember what you've learned about learning: you learn from repetition and first introductions are always awkward. The more you work with your thesaurus the better your ability to extract exactly what you need from it will become and you will grow mentally rich because of it. In the quest to learn any subject thesauri are valuable tools you should learn to use.

The key to learning how to use your thesaurus is reading the beginning sections of the book, which explain how it is organized and how best to use it.

Each publisher of a new edition thesaurus generally will organize their book a little differently than other publishers. There are of course many common elements contained in the structure of the thesauri. In most cases they are organized by grouping major subjects into headings, then those headings are generally divided by categories. Those categories are divided by parts of speech.

Understanding the system of indexing of words and terms, usually with numbers, is the key to thesauri use. They are too valuable a learning resource not to learn how to use. They not only increase one's vocabulary but also extend mental boundaries and frame of reference to words and terms. Thesauri provide a wealth of word ideas.

Encyclopedias

Encyclopedias are concise works that embrace just about every subject. They are comprehensive, providing glances at a broad spectrum of subjects and fields. There are basically two types of encyclopedias and both are arranged alphabetically. The most common are general subject encyclopedias, which treat broad knowledge areas in topical format on just about any subject you can imagine.

There are also specialized encyclopedias devoted strictly to a single subject or field. The preceding information regarding dictionaries also applies to encyclopedias. An encyclopedia is often the beginning point for researching a subject or field with which you are not familiar or have only a cursory knowledge. Encyclopedias provide a sound foundation of general understanding upon which to build and expand.

All the research and reference tools we have discussed work to build your base of knowledge and understanding, starting from the word and proceeding through terms, subjects, concepts and fields. Expanded comprehension is what we seek for you as the base from which to master any subject you chose to learn. Follow the same format with those learning tools that you followed and performed in your Formal Reading Exercises.

Honorable Mention

There are available English Grammar and Style reference books formatted as general text, dictionaries, thesauri, and encyclopedias. In order for you to most effectively work with the word in English, we highly recommend the purchase or at minimum the usage of those reference materials. Advance your knowledge of the word by advancing your correct usage of English, and all the rules that apply. The long-term payoff is astronomical.

Remember in all that you do to learn how to learn. Be patient with yourself, take your time when reading, elect to strive for perfection in learning rather then speed your way to mediocre. What you have undertaken is a lifelong process.

Systems of Organized Information

Sources of information on everything known are plentiful, but plentiful does not mean accurate or truthful. Examine all the information that comes your way and don't be quick to accept all sources as authoritative. Keep an open but guarded mind.

There are however some very good sources of information that we can consult to increase our understanding in learning specific subjects and fields. Let's discuss several of those sources and see what they offer.

Almanacs

Almanacs are not just for farmers. They provide information far beyond agriculture. Generally published on a yearly basis, almanacs are great sources of current up-to-date information. Some almanacs are devoted to specialized topics and fields while others give more general information. They are generally brief in the information they offer and provide in most cases pointed statistical data.

Bibliographies

Bibliographies are a library reference desk in a book. They contain sources where you can find information. Some provide just lists of information or data, others are more detailed in their information. They cover most topics, and can be formatted to present past or current information. As a research tool bibliographies are also an excellent starting point because they direct your attention to a wide range of information sources on the given topic of interest.

Biographical Sources

Biographic source materials are not books on the life of some past or current figure but do provide information on people, past and current. They can focus on professional listings, historical figures, or people in the pop art world. They vary in length of information from a one-line sentence to almost full-scale biographies. Biographical indexes list additional reference sources, saving research time and effort. More biographical source materials are found in biographic dictionaries and biographic encyclopedias.

Directories

Generally, directories are lists of people, places, groups, or organizations, and often provide contact information. They cover a wide range of specific or general information on subjects, professions, fields, schools, and about anything your mind can dream up.

Manuals

Manuals are the "how to do" source of information. They are wonderful learning tools for an enormous range of subjects. They are specific and factual instruction guides.

Statistical Reference Sources

When only numbers will suffice, statistical sources save the day. Using numbers, someone somehow has taken the time to convert everything imaginable into a statistical fact. There are statistics on statistics, and the depth and breath of available sources is large.

There are many more information reference sources than those listed here. The system of organized information is very broad and encompasses all subjects. Our aim is to ensure that you know the most realizable and most commonly used sources. Local and Internet libraries are great places to begin any quest for information. Information can be found almost anywhere; it's the quality of that information that is so very important. The most essential action for you to commit yourself to at this stage of your mental development is to read constantly. Read what you think you're not interested in learning as well as what you may like and want to learn. In time you shall realize that all knowledge gained eventually finds usefulness in your life.

> "Words are real living miracles. When you work with words, the words work with you. When you work on words, the words work on you. When you embrace words, you and words become one."

4
Make Mathematics Easy

We remain with the same common sense logic approach toward mathematics that we have taken throughout this book to learn all other subjects: start with the word, not the numbers.

All subjects have rules that must be mastered, especially mathematics. The focus of our approach is to concentrate on the words and written word rules. Build your comprehension of mathematics first by building your general vocabulary, then by building your vocabulary of the language of the subject, and finally by building your understanding of the broader word definitions that are expressed as symbols. Once you have mastered those realities, then begin to learn the work of figuring out problems expressed in numbers and symbols. Mathematics will become far easier to learn when you know and understand the rules before you try to work the numbers.

Place your learning focus on the words, rules, symbols, and the specific language associated with the branch of mathematics you are learning, and build your mental mathematics structure one floor at a time.

Mathematics has a lot of rules, and they are generally taught in conjunction with working the numbers. That approach can lead to mental confusion and memory overload for the average person like me. Those among us who are underprivileged often live in environments full of mental and emotional burdens. Like so many young people in our inner cities and poorest rural areas, they may approach their learning situations while suffering from emotional overload factors. Again, one size does not fit all in the universe of learning. Maybe for you there are other factors that have mathematics as being difficult in your thoughts.

Regardless of past experience with learning the subject, take the single focused approach now. Build at your own natural rate of growth with the words of mathematics; then facility with the numbers and mastery of the subject will be attained.

Mathematics is simply the use of numbers as replacements for a lot of written words to reach resolution of a problem. Every subject comes back to the word as its foundation.

Symbols in mathematics came into use a long time ago to reduce the amount of handwritten words needed to express different operations. While that was necessary, it has also complicated learning the subject. All the so-called "complicated" subjects boil down to a large volume of words whose operational performance must be known exactly.

"I have just completed reading **The Miracle Learning System!**™ *with great interest as we are in the business of selling and teaching accounting software to small business owners. Accounting terminology is one of the more difficult subjects for small business owners to grasp. We like the systematic and structured approach of* **The Miracle Learning System!**™ *The use and maintenance of reading periods enables the reader to gauge their progress. The act of recording and maintaining the various legal pad lists, and methods for follow-up provides a feeling of accomplishment exactly like setting goals and then achieving them. We believe your methodology will be highly productive for individuals who wish to master specific subject matter for tests such as GED, SAT, licenses, foreign language, etc. We are looking forward to your computer software version".*

Henry W. Jenkins, MBA, CMA —
Micros & Business Solutions, Owner
West Hills, California

It is not the math that is complicated, rather it is all the rules and procedures that must be followed in math that are complicated, because they are locked away in symbols. Rules are difficult to learn when you're also trying to work the number representations of those rules from a limited understanding of the words.

Finding The Path

There are many mathematics libraries devoted exclusively to the subject. Within those libraries are to be found far more detailed and extensive works on mathematical terms than you're apt to find within your general-purpose local libraries.

There are literally tons of different dictionaries of mathematical terms and dictionaries of number words. There are mathematic encyclopedias and reference materials that provide instruction from the earliest known to the most current uses of many of the words and symbols used in math.

If your interest is in helping a small child learn mathematics, you'll find many easy to understand books on the language of mathematics that are devoted to grades K through 8 and upward, also math glossaries for children. Child level math glossaries are not a bad place for anyone to start to refresh math skill.

There are many different types of books available that start with the word as the focus.

The focus at the universities of YKT and YDRT for learning the words of mathematics first, is the best starting method.

If you don't have home access to the Internet, go to your local library and use theirs to perform a search on mathematics libraries. You're going to spend a lot of hours reading about all that is available to you on so many websites. While you are at the computer, perform another search on library reference sources. The information you learn from that second search will be very valuable to you in identifying resources to assist in your discovery of materials related to learning the words and language of other subjects for which you may have an interest.

The following are some personal favorite websites for math:

1. University of Cambridge, U.K. "Math Thesaurus; http://thesaurus.math.org/mmkb/view.html

2. Math Dictionary for Kids; www.amathsdictionaryforkids.com

3. Lycos Zone: Mathematics (vast amount of word based math info); www.Cut-the-knot.com/reciprocaloth.html

4. Drexel University: The Math Forum; http://mathforum.org

After you start looking at what's available on the Internet, you'll find your own favorite sites based on your needs and interest.

Use The System

The main library generally has a greater quantity of reference books than are found at local branches. In order to perform the reading exercises in your reference books, you're going to need to purchase your own copies of those books you find most interesting and valuable.

Each reference book you discover during your research at the library will have publisher's information on the inside front cover. The back cover of the book will have an ISBN number. Write that information down and take it to your nearest book store. Request that they order the book(s) for you using their "books in print" data. If the books are no longer in print the bookstore may be able to acquire them for you by other means.

There are also discount book retailers on the Internet that can supply those books for you when provided with the above information. Amazon.com is one Internet source;

also you can research within the Internet yellow pages for the contact information for publishers. When you call the publisher to arrange for your purchase, be sure to have the name of the book, the name of the author, and the date of publication. All of that information should also be printed on the inside front cover page of the book. When you cannot find a phone number for the publisher, write a letter requesting ordering information for the book.

Once you have gathered the books and other materials that provide instruction on the language of the branch of mathematics you have chosen, and the word and symbol definitions for that branch, continue to follow the methods you performed in Chapters 2 and 3 which taught you how to read your study books and perform the Formal Reading Exercises.

Keep your focus on building your understanding of the words, their pronunciation, definition, and correct spelling. Build your vocabulary with the terms each word or group of words means and represents.

Memorize the word meanings for the symbols for which you learn the definition or operational functionality related to the language of the subject.

Once you have reached your confidence level working at your own rate of speed, buy a textbook on that subject and start working the numbers.

> *You're going to be amazed at how fast you "get it" and how much quicker your comprehension enables you to work the numbers.*

In addition to any other reference books on mathematics you purchase, two books you'll need in your personal library are a high quality dictionary of symbols and a high quality encyclopedia of symbols. Both of those books will be valuable tools that will greatly aid in your ability to achieve understanding and comprehension of the rules and the operational functionality imbedded within mathematical symbols.

> "Words are real living miracles. When you work with words, the words work with you. When you work on words, the words work on you. When you embrace words, you and words become one."

5
Road Map to Your Own Personal Genius

The major components and subcomponents needed to construct your own mental skyscraper are listed below. The development plan for building your intellect from its foundation to the highest heights, one floor at a time is your responsibility. You are the architect that designs your mental structure. The look, style, form, capacity, and utility of your mental structure are in your hands. The finished product can be as broad or narrow as the fields of your interests and concerns in life.

There are no limits for you in your mental development. You can learn at your own rate and speed whatever subjects your heart and mind desire.

> Within the pages of this book you have learned what are the most important elements for success achievement, and been given a road map clearly directing you to where you elect to take yourself.

The order of focus in which the following is listed has great importance, and should be followed strictly in the future as you design your own personal learning curriculum.

Every human being in possession of his or her natural five senses is equal in learning potential. The key for learning has always been the design and control of the total environmental conditions for your learning circumstance.

You are now in control of that environment, and the filters that screen the information you receive. You are now free from the burdens of psychological weights and artificial barriers regarding your attainment of mental excellence.

The only limit to your mental growth is the time and effort put forth toward mental development.

In the Creation of all that exist on Earth, the human being has been given the unique miracle of mental growth. It is arguably the greatest of all the miracles, and the birthright of each human being is to learn and to grow to mental excellence.

The life we live, no matter what life that may be, is primarily about learning. Our condition in this life is fundamentally controlled by what we know and what we don't know.

The force field of that portion of our destiny controlled by our own free will is equal in strength to the effort we place in creating our own mental miracle.

It matters not who likes or dislikes that you have chosen to mentally grow, what matters is that you do it, that you strive with complete determination, that you never ever doubt nor disbelieve in your ability to learn.

May the Creator of the human mind grant to you and your mind His choicest Blessings on your straight path to mental growth.

Road Map
Character Development & Redevelopment:

1. New attitude development and modification.

2. Development of proper work ethic and values.

3. Right-minded thinking.

Train the self methods:

1. Establish comfort with your learning nature.

2. Think positive in acceptance of struggle.

3. Daily repetition and verbal affirmations.

4. Use of the five senses.

5. Consistent effort.

6. Organized thinking exercises.

7. Right-minded thinking exercises.

8. Applied self-determined exercises.

Learning Foundation & Rudiments:

1. Work with the word and build a large vocabulary.

2. Understand every word you read.

3. Use progress measurement techniques.

4. Maintain levelheaded thinking.

Train the self-methods:

1. Invest in high-quality dictionaries.

2. Learn beginning sections of the dictionary.

3. Read books on new, difficult and unknown subjects.

4. Highlight all unknown words and track all words not found in your dictionary.

5. Learn the correct pronunciation, definition, and spelling of unknown words.

6. Track the total time of each Reading Period.

7. Read slowly and complete each Reading Period at your own rate of speed.

8. Complete the five Formal Reading Exercises on all new subjects.

9. Measure your learning progress after completion of each exercise.

10. Guard your mind against subtle seduction from negatives.

Advanced Learning Methods:

1. Learn the language of each subject.

2. Learn the systems of how knowledge is organized.

3. Rely on the organized sources of the word.

4. Learn the correct usage of English grammar and style.

5. Understand the systems of information sources.

Train the self methods:

1. Learn expanded and multiple word terms, subject terms, and concepts.

2. Learn the groupings — categories and other divisions of knowledge areas.

3. Learn the types and formats of dictionaries, glossaries of terms, thesauri, and encyclopedias.

4. Learn how information is organized and used as reference materials.

Math Made Easy:

1. Learn the words of math before learning to figure the numbers.

2. Comprehend the worded rules for each math subject.

3. Learn the meanings of words that math symbols represent.

Train the self-methods:

1. Use the libraries and Internet to locate mathematics libraries to find instruction books on math subjects.

2. Acquire books with worded instructions on the rules of math.

3. Acquire a dictionary and encyclopedia of math symbols.

4. Master the words of math then work the numbers, figures, and symbols.

In conclusion, know that the genius is home. Knock and the door will be opened.

> "Words are real living miracles. When you work with words, the words work with you. When you work on words, the words work on you. When you embrace words, you and words become one."

Afterword

Be! — It is my sincere hope that you will commit to a life of self-cultivation with determined consistency in learning. The world is in need of your good mind and contributions. Please share with me your thoughts on how this book can be improved to help others. I'd really like to know all the ways this book has helped you, and please include permission to publish your remarks. Address your letters to me at:

AMM Publishing Company
Attn: Aamir
P.O. Box 846
Lawrence, Kansas 66044-0846

There is nothing more rewarding to me than seeing improvement ever evolving within myself, and in others. Peradventure this book will introduce that process into your life, for the remainder of your life.

With Sincere Gratitude,

Aamir M. Muhammad

"Words are real living miracles. When you work with words, the words work with you. When you work on words, the words work on you. When you embrace words, you and words become one."

Appendix

Year 2005 - 2006 Research Project
Opportunity for Teachers

AMM Publishing Company is currently designing a research project that focuses on high school and freshman college students in the ninth, tenth, and eleventh grade-levels. The purpose of the project is to systematically measure, record, and document student outcomes using *The Miracle Learning System!*™.

The research project will be national in scope, and twelve (12) urban inner city test sites and twelve (12) rural community test sites shall be selected to conduct the research project. Only one site location will be selected for any one inner city, or rural community.

Qualified teachers interested in becoming research facilitators should write a letter to the address below. Please include your certification and years of teaching experience, description of proposed research site noting whether urban or rural, proposed number of students that would be included in the research, and any suggestions regarding the design of the research project. All cost and materials needed to perform the research shall be provided by AMM Publishing Company.

Year 2005 - 2006 Research Project
AMM Publishing Company
P.O. Box 846
Lawrence, Kansas 66044-0846

THE WORD UP PROGRAM™
For
Corporations – Foundations – Benefactors

THE WORD UP PROGRAM™'s objective is to provide free copies of *The Miracle Learning System!*™ to four categories of the underprivileged population throughout America. The primary target beneficiaries of the program are:

✦ Tenth grade high school students located in urban and rural low-income areas.
✦ College freshmen.
✦ Students that have dropped out of high school.
✦ Inmates in juvenile detention centers and prisons.
✦ Special Education students who drop out.

THE WORD UP PROGRAM™ is a Direct Impact way for corporate America, foundations and private individual benefactors to practice good citizenship by providing cogent support to help save students entering high school and college, and to help rescue those that have dropped out, in communities with historically poor learning skills.

AMM Publishing Company is on a mission to get *The Miracle Learning System!*™ book in the hands of every person whose life it may improve. If you would like to help spread the word about this program, or to have your corporation, foundation, or service organization participate, please write to us for more detailed information at:

WORD UP PROGRAM™
AMM Publishing Company
P.O. Box 846
Lawrence, Kansas 66044-0846

Professional Services

Aamir M. Muhammad is available to present the following professional services. To schedule him for your up coming event, or to have Aamir consult with your organization, contact: AMM Publishing Company at our toll free phone number: 1-800-315-7899 and ask for the professional services scheduler.

Speaking Engagements:

Conferences
Corporate Retreats
Special Events for Organizations
Education Programs
Faith-Based Programs
Colleges and Universities

Public Appearances:

Guest for Television and Radio Talk Shows
State Fairs
Trade and Specialty Shows
High Schools

Consulting Services:

Curriculum Inclusion and Implementation of T*he Miracle Learning System!*™

Seminars and Workshops

AMM Publishing Company sponsors seminars and workshops featuring Aamir M. Muhammad and T*he Miracle Learning System!*™ beginning in calendar year 2005. Visit our website at http://www.ammpublishing.com to find the schedule of dates and times in your area.

AMM Publishing Scholarship Program

AMM Publishing believes that giving back to our readership is a proper obligation of good corporate citizenry. As is the case with our inaugural publication of *The Miracle Learning System!*™, AMM Publishing selects 12 students to receive scholarships equal to one percent (1%) of the net sales, including reprints, from all of our publications.

Each scholarship recipient receives four (4) quarterly checks per year for the life of sales of that individual book. Revised editions of any title do not apply to selected students. Twelve new students are selected for any revised editions published under an existing book title.

AMM Publishing is planning a merchandise collection in the near future. Continue to watch for announcements on our website at ammpublishing.com. Each annual collection of merchandise sold by AMM Publishing shall be included in our scholarship program.

Students in grades K-12 are eligible for selection. Send letters of interest to AMM Publishing and tell us about your nominee.

AMM Publishing Company
Attention: Scholarships Program
P.O. Box 846
Lawrence, Kansas 66044-0846

Index

A

Advanced learning method 43–56
    dictionaries in 46–48
    encyclopedias in 51–52
    glossaries of terms in 48–49
    and language of subjects 44
    and organized sources of words 46
    and organized systems of knowledge 45
    and systems of organized information 53
    thesauri in 50–55

Affirmations 6–9

Almanacs 53

Antonyms 50

Applied Self-Determination exercises 9

Attitude 1 (See also Mental preparation)

B

Bibliographies 53

Biographical sources 54

Books, purchasing 13, 60–61, 63

C

Canada, Damon 9

Children, math resources for 60–61

Closet exercise 6–8

Cultivation of the mind 5–6

D

Dahms, Douglas M. 44

Definitions 19, 44

Deliberate action 26

Dictionaries 11–13
    basic word usage 46–47
    biographic 54
    elements of 14
    at library 25
    looking up words in 25–26, 30, 33, 38–39
    mathematical 60
    new words not found in 20, 25
    preliminary reading of 13
    reading exercise with 22
    subject 47–48
    of symbols 47, 63

Directories 54

Discipline 29–30, 40

Dress Right exercise 8–9

E

Encyclopedias 51–152, 60, 63

F

Fears about learning 29

First introductions 3

Formal Reading Exercises 15
    Exercise 1 16–25
    Exercise 2 26–30
    Exercise 3 30–33

Exercise 4 33–37
Exercise 5 38–39

Foundations for learning 35–37

G

Glossaries 48–49, 60

Growth (See also Mental growth)
   in learning mathematics 58
   patterns of xvi
   preparation for 1, 36–37

I

Informal reading exercises 22–23

Information, organized systems of 53–55

Internet 61–63

J

Jefferson, Thomas vi

Jenkins, Henry W. 59

Jordan, Brian C. xix

K

Knowledge, organized systems of 45

L

Language 44
   basic language dictionaries 47–48
   English grammar and style reference books 53–54
   of mathematics 60
   of specific subjects 43–55

Learning xv–xix
   advanced approach to 43–55
   and condition in life 66
   foundations for 35–37
   by hearts vs. by memory 5
   improvement in 29
   of mathematics 57–63
   personal curriculum for 65–70
   of subject language 43–55
   of unknown words 18–21, 25

Levelheaded thinking 32–33

Libraries 25, 55, 59–60

M

Manuals 54

Mathematics 57–63
   libraries devoted to 59–61
   resources for learning 59–63
   road map for learning 67–70
   rules for mastery of 57, 59
   subject dictionaries for 47
   symbols in 58

Mental Elevation Markers 28–30, 32

Mental growth 30, 32, 36–37, 65–70

Mental preparation 1–10
   Applied Self-Determination exercises for 9
   Closet exercise for 6–8
   cultivation of the mind 5–6
   Dress Right exercise for 8–9
   and facts about learning 3–5

The Miracle Learning System!™ xv–xix

Muhammad, Tasha xvii

O

Organization 5–8
    of information systems 53
    of sources of words 46
    of systems of knowledge 45

P

Personal learning curriculum 65–70

Physical action (for mental preparation) 6, 8, 10

Preliminary reading exercises 22–23

Pronunciation 19

R

Reading comprehension 29–30, 35, 40

Reading exercises 13
    analyzing results of 28–30
    defined 16–18
    formal 15 (See also Formal Reading Exercises)
    informal 22–23
    for learning math 61
    learning of unknown words in 18–21, 25
    materials required for 14–15
    performance instructions for 16
    reduction in time needed for 40
    subject for 14
    time periods for 15
    use of dictionary in 19

use of highlighter markers in 18, 26–28, 30–35, 38–39
   use of legal pads in 16–17, 18, 21, 28–30

Reading Periods 15–18, 21, 40

Reading speed 32–33, 38

Reagan, Ronald 3

Repetition 3–4, 6, 8–9, 20

Right action 8–9

Road map for mental growth 67–70

S

Scholarship program 76

Senses 5

Spelling 20

Statistical reference sources 54–55

Subject dictionaries 46–47

Subjects:
   language of 43–55
   organized sources of words related to 46–53
   organized systems of knowledge about 45
   rules for mastery of 57
   systems of organized information about 53–55

Symbols, mathematics 58–63

Synonyms 50

T

Thesauri 50–51

Thinking:
   and cultivation of mind 5–6
   exercises for correcting 6–10
   levelheaded 32–33
   and power of thoughts 4

Trade associations 48

U

Universities of YKT and YDRT xviii–13, 42

Unknown words:
   added to vocabulary 29
   highlighting 18, 26–28, 30–35, 38–39
   learning process for 17–21, 25–26
   not found in dictionary 20–25

V

Vocabulary 36–37, 57–58

W

Williams, Dan J. 36

Words xiv, xx, 10, 41, 56, 64, 70, 72

The Miracle Learning System! ™
Order Form

Please copy this Order Form and check the appropriate box for the type of order you are sending. When sending a gift order, please be sure to add the name and shipping address for the person you want to receive your gift. Please add your name and address in the buyer's section of this form. We will forward to you a confirmation upon shipping your order.

Check the Box for your order:

Ship to Buyer: ❑   Gift Order: ❑

Buyers Name: _____

Buyers Address: _____

City: _____ State: _____ Zip: _____

Number of copies: _____

Ship to (name): _____

Ship to (address): _____

City: _____ State: _____ Zip: _____

Gift Message: _____

Please send $14.95 per copy, plus $2.95 shipping per book.
Sorry, no COD orders.
Send Check or Money Order payable to:
AMM Publishing Company
P.O. Box 846
Lawrence, Kansas 66044-0846
Thank you!

Credit Card Order: (Check one only) VISA ❑   MASTERCARD ❑

Credit Card Number: _____

Name on Card: _____

Expiration date on card: _____

Authorized Signature: _____
(Must be name on card)

Credit Card Orders are also accepted on our website: www.amm-publishing.com or by calling our Toll Free Number: 1-800-315-7899

MAIL TO ADDRESS FOR ORDER FORM:

AMM Publishing Company
P.O. Box 846
Lawrence, Kansas 66044-0846